KID COACHES.
Make a Lemonade Stand Contest!

This Mentor's Guide and accompanying Student Workbook is designed to help you run a mini Lemonade Alley® Lemonade Stand Contest. The goal of this program is to teach kids that business is fun, creative and helpful.

At Lemonade Alley, we're looking for entrepreneurial heroes. Heroes who want to help kids make cool stuff. Heroes want to help kids support charities. If that's you, get your lemons on!

On behalf of the BizGym Foundation, I salute you for taking a leadership role in mentoring the Lemonade Alley challenge of *Profit to SHARE!*

Love, Lemons & Aloha,

Steve Sue
Chief Lemon Head, Lemonade Alley
LemonadeAlley.com | BizGym.org

© 2016, BizGym Foundation, a 501(c)(3) nonprofit. All Rights Reserved. | Version 2016

About Lemonade Alley

A Lemonade Stand Contest
Lemonade Alley is just a lemonade stand contest. As an event, it's a shopping mall of lemonade stands where kids build stands and sell lemonade in a head-to-head contest to see who can make the most for charity.

Scads of Preparation Exercises
The accompanying Student Workbook offers hands-on exercises to help teams build every part of their lemonade stand business. Workshops materials are offered in 3- and 10-session versions through the BizGym Foundation (BizGym.org) and Amazon.com.

THE GOAL: Your Mini Lemonade Alley
Run your own mini Lemonade Alley® Challenge at your school cafeteria, rec center, church or any youth organization. All you need is some space, tables, lemonade, kid signs and lots of smiles.

THE PRIZE: Free Trip to a Regional Run-Off
Winning teams from local events may go on to compete in regional Lemonade Alley events. You are invited to charge a "Lemonade Tax" on sales revenues to defray costs and provide funding for cash prizes and/or trips to regional events.

For Pictures & Ideas: **LemonadeAlley.com**

"... just a lemonade stand contest..."
2-5 Kids, Grades K-12:
1. Create a Recipe
2. Build a Stand
3. Sell for Charity

Kidpreneur Tools

"Lemonade Alley Kidpreneur Challenge"
Workbooks & Mentor Guides available at:
Amazon.com

Challenge Events
1. Your Local Mini Event
2. Regional Run-Offs

BizGym Foundation
LemonadeAlley.com
BizGym.org

Running a Lemonade Stand Contest

It's Easy!
This Guide and accompanying workbook contain everything you need to prepare teams and run a lemonade stand contest in your teaching environment. While this system contains many specific exercises, it's just a lemonade stand contest. Feel free to improvise!

Lemonade Logistics
Mini events can be simple to complex. The simplest version to have teams garnish generic lemonade provided by your organization. You can be fancier by letting teams create their own recipes. And instead of simple hand-made signs, you could let teams build full lemonade stands.

Securing Approvals
Check early to secure pre-approvals to hold a lemonade Alley event. If you encounter doubters, just give them a reason to say "yes!" For example, "Don't you want your kids to learn essential life skills? Aren't you interested in offering hands-on, project-based learning? Don't you want to be ahead of the educational curve?" Be positive and illustrate the value that kids will gain.

Event Checklists
Checklists and instructions on how to run a contest are included at the end of this Guide.

For Pictures & Ideas: **LemonadeAlley.com**

"...it's just a lemonade stand contest. Feel free to improvise!"

Event Options
1. Teams Garnish Only
2. Custom Team Recipes

Reasons to Approve
1. Learn essential life skills
2. Hands-On Learning
3. Project-based Learning
4. Ahead of the curve

BizGym Foundation
LemonadeAlley.com
BizGym.org

Contents

Workshop Exercises
To Prepare Teams for a Lemonade Stand Contest

1. Build Your Team
2. Create a Big Idea
3. Invent Your Product
4. Create an Up-Sell Product
5. Make a Business Plan
6. Make a Menu
7. Perfect Your Process
8. Make Your Marketing
9. Create Your Pitch
10. Test, Tweak & Tweet

Lemonade Alley Event

Event Day Forms

Preparation Materials

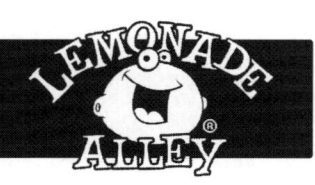

Program Goals
This program is designed to teach youth (grades K-12) the arts of innovation, entrepreneurship and financial literacy. Program goals include encouraging youth to explore innovation and creative skills, understand that business can be fun and rewarding, and learn the positive values of *"Profit to SHARE"* by supporting worthy causes.

Hands-On Activities
This workbook contains hands-on exercises for teams to prepare for a Lemonade Alley event. While exercises are grouped into a 10-session format, you may alter the schedule or assign exercises as homework to meet time constraints.

Flexible Materials
Each session section in this Mentor's Guide features preparation notes, materials list, session options and mentoring tips. You're welcome to schedule exercises and session time length to fit your needs.

Ready? Let's Begin!

"Profit to SHARE..."
Goals Include:
1. Innovation Skills
2. Entrepreneurship
3. Financial Literacy
4. Positive Biz Values

Fun Activities
1. Hands-On Assignments
2. Team Projects
3. Homework Option

Flexible Sessions
Customize any of these:
1. Session Scheduling
2. Number of Sessions
3. Exercises
4. Session Time Length

S1: Introduction & Team-Building

Session Length: 2 hours (variable)

Session Goals
- Introduce Lemonade Alley
- Set Teams & Positions
- Introduce Your Charity

Preparation
- Mentor's Guide
- Workbooks (1 per team)
- Pencils, Coloring Pens, Blunt Scissors
- Pre-Select Charity & % Donation
- Pre-set Lemonade Alley event day, time and location

Options
- Invite Charity Representative
- Invite Executive or Team-Building Expert
- Plastic holders for team name tags

1A. INTRODUCE LEMONADE ALLEY (30 mins)
- **Introduce the Program:** prepare teams for a Lemonade Alley local event.
- **Play Lemonade Alley YouTube Video:** https://youtu.be/eEqb1Qpcjig (also at lemonadealley.com).

S1

1B. "HOW IT WORKS" PAGE
- **Log Mentor Name:** have students write your name on How It Works page.
- **Log Local Event Details:** have students write Day, Date, Time, Location.
- **Explain Regional Lemonade Alley Event in Honolulu:** prize for a team to go on to the regional event.

1C. MAKE STUDENT TEAMS (60 mins)
- **Team-Building Expert:** Present the roles of President, Treasurer, Maker, Marketer and Server (all described on name tags on Build a Team page).
- **Teams of 5:** break up students into groups of 5.
- **TIP!** You can breakup students any way you wish. Some draft Presidents, others count off students by team numbers and yet others allow students to pick their own teams of friends.
- **Team Positions:** members select team positions.
- **Team Name Tags:** teams personalize name tags. Colorful is fine. Draft version fine. A final version can be made later from clean form at end of workbook.
- **OPTIONS:** provide plastic holders. Have teams wear at workshops.
- **EVENT DAY NOTE:** Name tags to be worn at Lemonade Alley events.

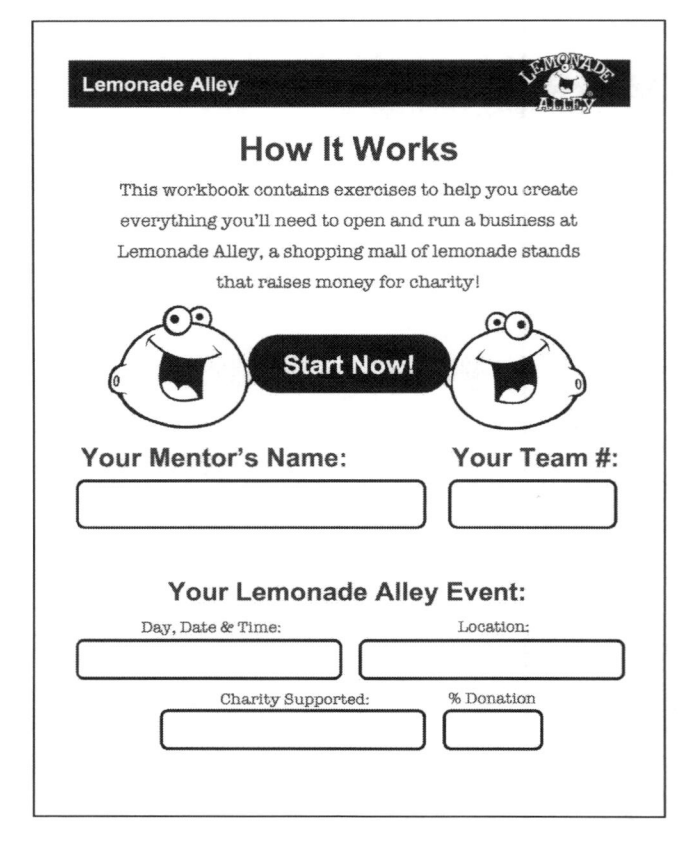

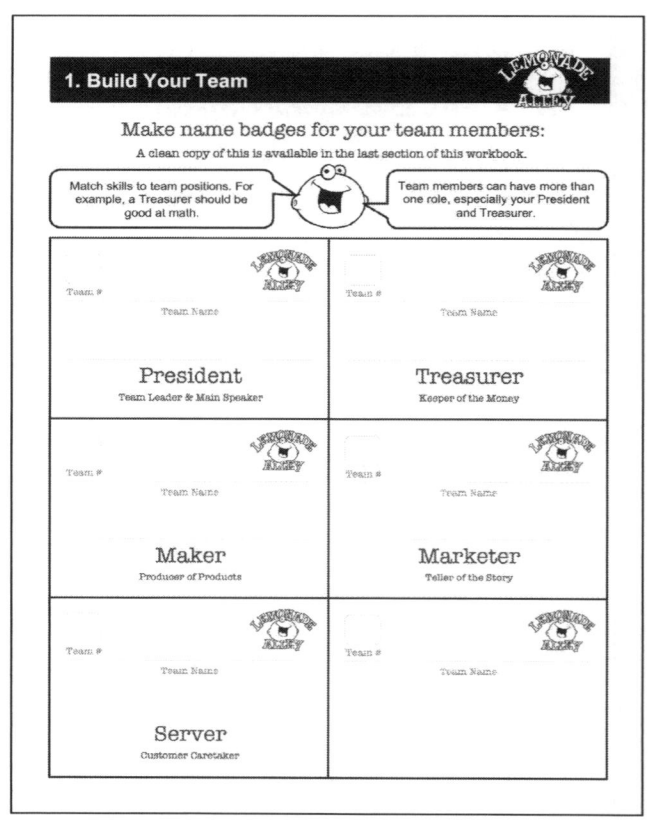

Lemonade Alley

How It Works

This workbook contains exercises to help you create everything you'll need to open and run a business at Lemonade Alley, a shopping mall of lemonade stands that raises money for charity!

Start Now!

Your Mentor's Name:

Your Team #:

Your Lemonade Alley Event:
Day, Date & Time:

Location:

Charity Supported:

% Donation

---

1. Build Your Team

Make name badges for your team members:

A clean copy of this is available in the last section of this workbook.

Match skills to team positions. For example, a Treasurer should be good at math.

Team members can have more than one role, especially your President and Treasurer.

Team # — Team Name	Team # — Team Name
President — Team Leader & Main Speaker	**Treasurer** — Keeper of the Money
Maker — Producer of Products	**Marketer** — Teller of the Story
Server — Customer Caretaker	

1D. KNOW YOUR CHARITY (30 mins)
- **Charity Representative:** present charity's cause and mission. Website, video, brochures, stickers and other charity SWAG welcome. Discuss % Donation to Charity and teams to log on How It Works page.
- **Log Charity Information:** students to log key information about charity.
- **Write Your Charity a Note:** each student to write the charity a note. The goal is to raise student awareness of the charity's work and start establishing a relationship with the charity.

Collect Charity Notes & Send, Collect Name Tags

Choose Your Charity

Name the charity your team will support:

Who do they help?

Write your charity a note saying why you want to raise money for them.

Make sure to let your charity know you're playing for them. They might even want to help!

S2: Create Your Big Idea

Session Length: 2 hours (variable)

Session Goals
- Create Main Business Idea & Theme
- Create Company Name & Slogan
- Create a Main Sign for Lemonade Stand

Preparation
- Large Cardboard (1 per team)
- Pencils, Color Pens, Blunt Scissors

Options
- Invite a Naming Expert (an advertising, marketing or writing expert).
- Invite a Design Expert (a store designer, graphic designer or architect).
- Additional Mentors OK in work segments.

2A. NAME & SLOGAN (60 mins)
- **Naming Expert Presentation:** give tips & demo on how to make name & slogan.
- **Presidents to Lead:** Team presidents to lead development of team name and slogan. Log content in workbooks.
- **Presidents Present:** president to present and explain company name and slogan.

2B. LEMONADE SIGN (60 mins)
- **Design Expert Presentation:** give tips & demo on how to design a main sign.
- **Distribute Art Supplies**
- **Marketers to Lead:** Team marketer to lead development of a main sign.
- **Marketers Present:** marketer to present and explain main sign.

Collect Signs for Use at Event

---

2. Create Your Big Idea

President: lead creating your lemonade stand name.

Your Charity?   Your Recipe?   Your Customers?   Your Sponsor?

Create your company name:

Explain how your name tells your business story:

Create a slogan:

"Just Do It"   "Think Different"   "Profit to Share!"

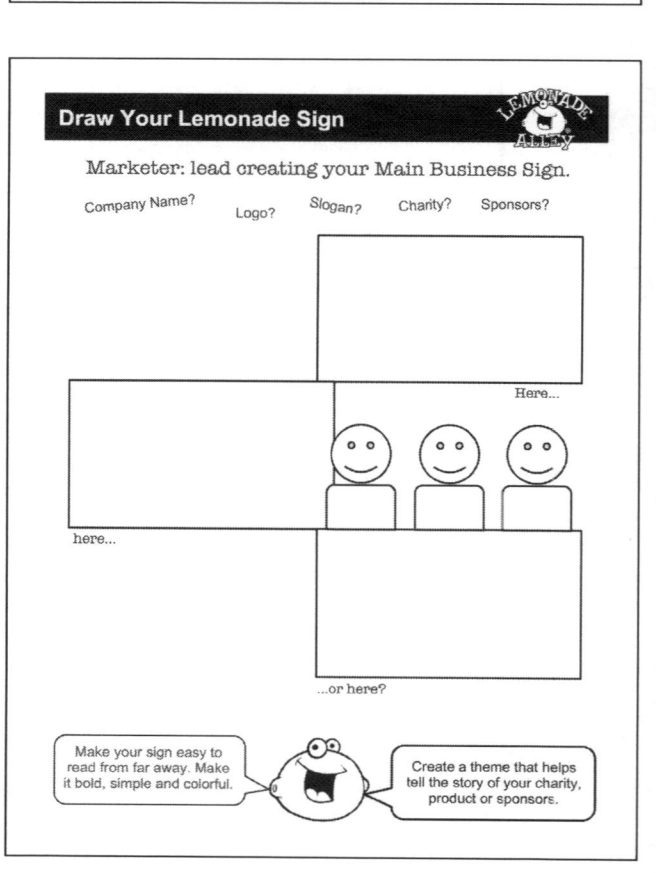

Your lemonade stand name should be fun to attract customers.

Make your lemonade stand cool with a theme like mad scientists. Or make it tell your charity's story.

Draw Your Lemonade Sign

Marketer: lead creating your Main Business Sign.

Company Name?   Logo?   Slogan?   Charity?   Sponsors?

Here...

here...

...or here?

Make your sign easy to read from far away. Make it bold, simple and colorful.

Create a theme that helps tell the story of your charity, product or sponsors.

S3: Invent Your Product

Session Length: 2 hours (variable)

Session Goals
- Certify Food Safety
- Create a Lemonade Recipe
- Create a Cup Presentation

Preparation
- Provide Lemonade (powdered OK)
- Provide Cups (very small tasters best)
- Decoration/Ingredient Garnishes (fruit, candy, straws etc.)

Options
- Invite a Chef (many chefs can provide lemonade and ingredients).
- Additional Mentors OK in work segments.

3A. FOOD SAFETY (30 mins)
- **Chef Presentation:** give tips & demo on how to be food safe.
- **Maker to Lead:** Team makers to lead team in passing Food Safety Test.
- **Maker Secures Food Safety Certificate:** a form at end of workbook. Must be displayed on booth during event day.

3B. INVENT YOUR RECIPE (30 mins)
- **Chef Presentation:** give tips & demo on how to create a healthy and tasty drink.
- **Maker to Lead:** Team makers to lead development of recipe. Instruct Makers to make recipes relate their story.
  HANDS-ON RECIPE DEVELOPMENT: optional depending upon available resources, time and cleanup conditions.

---

3. Food Safety Certificate

Maker: lead your team in passing this test.
Complete the clean copy at the end of this workbook. Display it on your lemonade stand.

A. Lemonade for sale must be made and served according to health laws. — YES or NO

B. Food and beverages made with heat (stoves, ovens, etc.) must be made and packaged in a certified commercial kitchen like a restaurant. — YES or NO

C. Pre-packaged food products can be sold at a lemonade stand if stored properly. — YES or NO

D. Hand gloves must be used at all times when preparing and serving lemonade. — YES or NO

E. Always wash hands, lemons and other ingredients before juicing or cutting. — YES or NO

F. If you've left your stand, when you come back, you must wash your hands before preparing or serving. — YES or NO

G. Keep all perishables in food-safe containers like coolers. — YES or NO

H. Never taste directly from serving tools or storage containers. — YES or NO

I. Excess liquids and ice cannot be dumped outside and instead must be taken home for disposal. — YES or NO

J. Animals and pets are not allowed to be present. — YES or NO

Always check local health, business and other government laws for latest requirements.

Answers: They're all "Yes"!

Invent Your Recipe

Maker: lead your team in making your recipe.
Create a recipe for use on Lemonade Alley Day. A clean copy is in the last section.

Pulp? Zest? Honey? Sugar? Agave? Stevia? Candy? Mint? Basil? Fresh Fruit? Ginger? Rosemary? Ice Cubes?

Can You Reduce Sugar?

Ingredients List:

Step-by-Step Instructions:

Try using lemon skin (called "zest") to get lemon flavor without having to use a lot of sugar.

S3

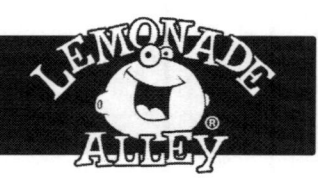

3C. CREATE YOUR PRESENTATION (45 mins)
- **Chef Presentation:** give tips & demo on how to present food in a restaurant environment as well as in a drink cup.
- **Maker to Lead:** Team makers to lead development of cup design. Instruct Makers to make cup designs relate their story.
  HANDS-ON RECIPE DEVELOPMENT: optional depending upon available resources, time and cleanup conditions.
- **Makers to Present:** makers to present and explain cup design.

3D. CREATE RECIPE CARD (15 mins)
- **Makers to Lead:** Team Makers to lead final draft of the recipe card that's available in back of the workbook. This card will need to be available in the team's lemonade stand on event day.
- **Teams Keep Recipe Cards:** teams can keep their recipe cards in their workbooks until event day.

S4: Create an Up-Sell Product

Session Length: 2 hours (variable)

Session Goals
- Create a complimentary product

Preparation
- Provide craft items (for arcade games, duct tape wallets, friendship bracelets and other arts and crafts can be made from donated materials)
- **WARNING:** Food is not legal if cooked & packaged outside of a commercial kitchen (lemonade is not cooked).

Options
- Invite a crafts expert (many art or crafts people can provide materials).
- Additional Mentors OK in work segments.

4A. CREATE UPSELL PRODUCT (120 mins)
- **Craft Expert Presentation:** give tips & demo on how to be creative and make attractive and safe products/services.
- **President to Lead:** Team presidents to lead creating up-sells that relate to the main idea of the team's business.
- **Presidents to present:** Presidents to present and explain up-sell products.

4B. CREATE UP-SELL CARD
- **Presidents to Lead:** Team Presidents to lead final draft of the up-sell card that's available in back of the workbook. This card will need to be available in the team's lemonade stand on event day.
- **Teams Keep Recipe Cards:** teams can keep their recipe cards in their workbooks until event day.

S5: Create a Business Plan

Session Length: 2 hours (variable)

Session Goals
- Understand Customers
- Set Sales Goals
- Learn Banking & Accounting
- Create a StoryTree® 1-Page Biz Plan

Preparation
- Provide picture magazines for cut outs.
- Provide pencils/pens, blunt scissors, tape/glue.

Options
- Invite a business expert.
- Additional Mentors OK in work segments.

5A. DEFINE CUSTOMERS (45 mins)
- **Business Expert Presentation:** give tips & demo on how to find best customers.
- **President to Lead:** Team presidents to lead creating defining best customers.
- **President to Present:** Presidents to present and explain target customers.

5B. CREATE SALES GOALS (30 mins)
- **Business Expert Presentation:** give tips & demo how to set sales goals.
- **Treasurer to Lead:** Team Treasurers to lead setting sales goals.
- **Treasurer to Present:** Treasurers to present and explain sales goals.

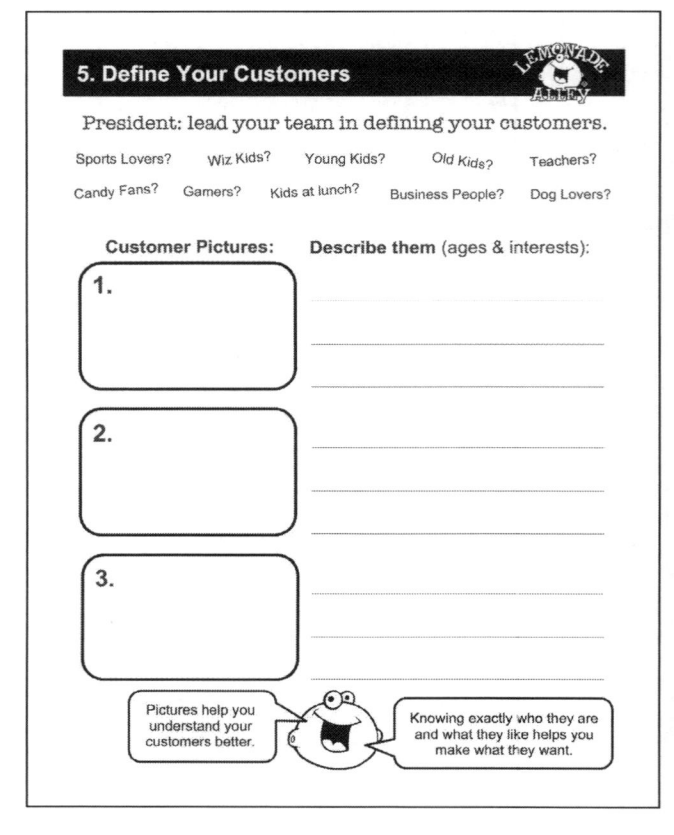

5C. PREPARE SALES FORM

- **Business Expert Presentation:** give tips & demo on how use the Sales Performance Form on event day.
- **Treasurer to Prepare:** Team Treasurers to prepare the Sales Performance Form in the back of the workbook by inserting Sales Goals.
- **Teams Keep Sales Performance Form:** teams can keep their form in their workbooks until event day.

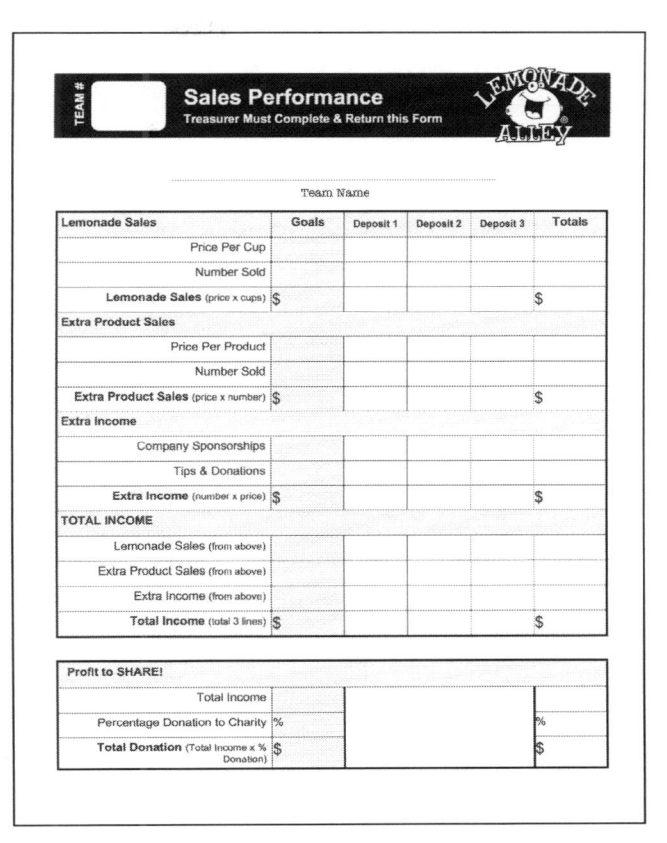

5D. PREPARE DEPOSIT TICKETS (15 mins)

- **Business Expert Presentation:** give tips & demo on how use the Deposit Tickets on event day.
- **Treasurer to Prepare:** Team Treasurers to prepare the Deposit Tickets Form. A clean copy of Deposit Tickets is in the back of the workbook for use on event day.
- **Teams Keep Deposit Tickets:** teams can keep their form in their workbooks until event day.

5E. CREATE STORYTREE® BIZ PLAN (30 mins)

- **Business Expert Presentation:** give tips & demo on how create a StoryTree 1-Page Business Plan.
- **President to Lead:** Team Presidents to lead the completion of the StoryTree Business Plan. A clean copy of the StoryTree is in the back of the workbook. Team StoryTree Biz Plans should be displayed on lemonade stands on event day.
- **Teams Keep StoryTree Biz Plans:** teams can keep their business plans in their workbooks until event day.

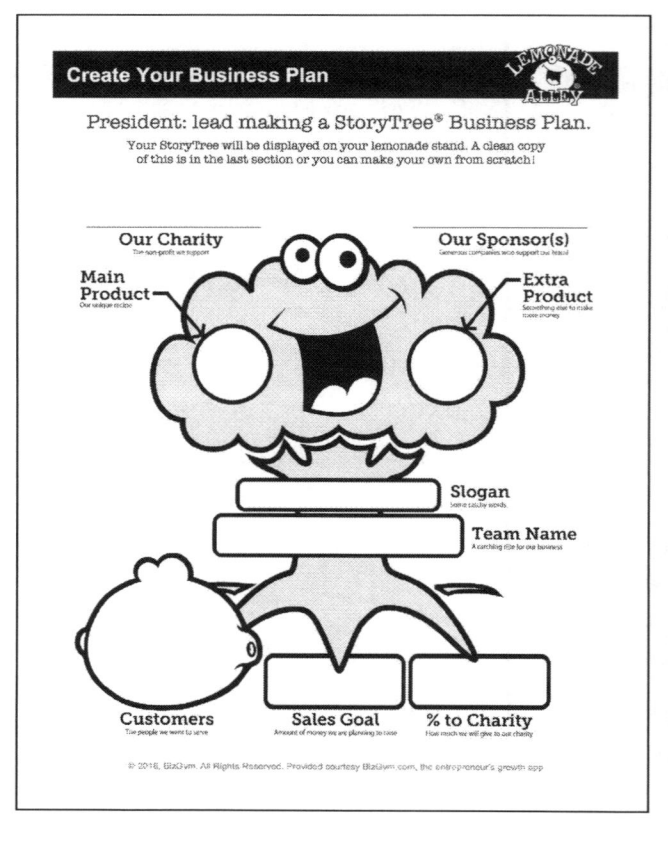

S6: Make a Menu

Session Length: 2 hours (variable)

Session Goals
- Create a Coupon Special
- Tweet Your Special
- Make a Menu

Preparation
- Provide paper, pencils/pens, blunt scissors.

Options
- Invite a marketing expert.
- Additional Mentors OK in work segments.

6A. CREATE A COUPON SPECIAL (40 mins)
- **Marketing Expert Presentation:** give tips & demo on how to create a special.
- **Marketer to Lead:** Team Marketers to lead creating a paper coupon special.
- **Marketer to Present:** Marketers to present and explain coupon.

6B. TWEET ABOUT YOUR SPECIAL (40 mins)
- **Marketing Expert Presentation:** give tips & demo how to tweet.
- **Marketer to Lead:** Team Marketers to lead all in creating tweets.
- **Marketer to Present:** Marketers to present and explain.

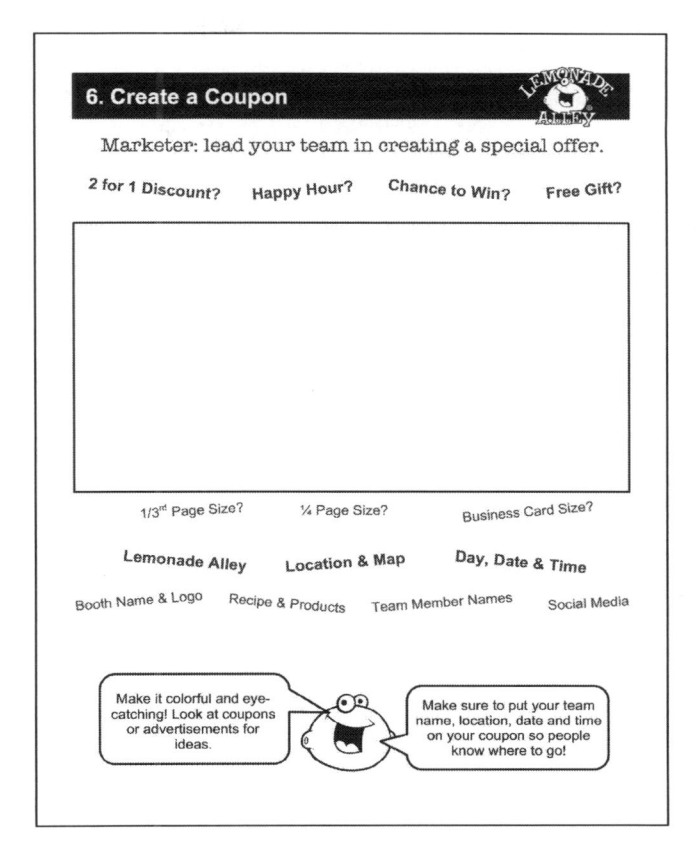

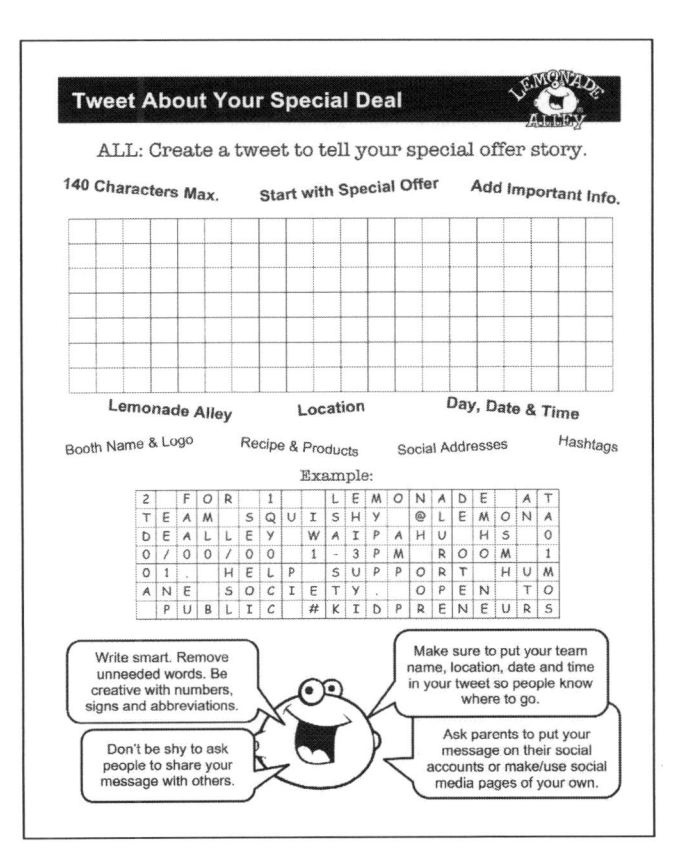

---

6. Create a Coupon
Marketer: lead your team in creating a special offer.

2 for 1 Discount? Happy Hour? Chance to Win? Free Gift?

1/3rd Page Size? ¼ Page Size? Business Card Size?

Lemonade Alley Location & Map Day, Date & Time

Booth Name & Logo Recipe & Products Team Member Names Social Media

Make it colorful and eye-catching! Look at coupons or advertisements for ideas.

Make sure to put your team name, location, date and time on your coupon so people know where to go!

Tweet About Your Special Deal
ALL: Create a tweet to tell your special offer story.

140 Characters Max. Start with Special Offer Add Important Info.

Lemonade Alley Location Day, Date & Time

Booth Name & Logo Recipe & Products Social Addresses Hashtags

Example:

2	F	O	R	1		L	E	M	O	N	A	D	E		A	T
T	E	A	M		S	Q	U	I	S	H	Y		@	L	E	M	O	N	A
D	E	A	L	L	E	Y		W	A	I	P	A	H	U		H	S		O
0	/	0	0	/	0	0		1	-	3	P	M		R	O	O	M		1
0	1	.		H	E	L	P		S	U	P	P	O	R	T		H	U	M
A	N	E		S	O	C	I	E	T	Y	.		O	P	E	N		T	O
	P	U	B	L	I	C		#	K	I	D	P	R	E	N	E	U	R	S

Write smart. Remove unneeded words. Be creative with numbers, signs and abbreviations.

Don't be shy to ask people to share your message with others.

Make sure to put your team name, location, date and time in your tweet so people know where to go.

Ask parents to put your message on their social accounts or make/use social media pages of your own.

6C. CREATE YOUR MENU (40 mins)

- **Marketing Expert Presentation:** give tips & demo on how create great menu.
- **Server to Lead:** Team Servers to lead the creation of menu on 8 1/2" x 11" paper. Color encouraged. Stand-up frames encouraged.
- **Server to Present:** Server to present and explain team Menu.

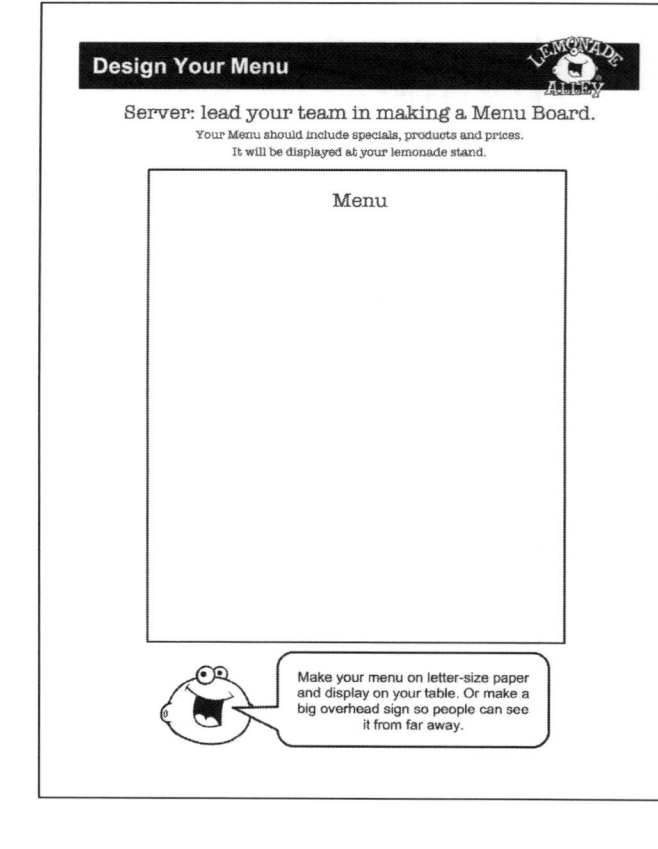

Design Your Menu

Server: lead your team in making a Menu Board.

Your Menu should include specials, products and prices.
It will be displayed at your lemonade stand.

Menu

Make your menu on letter-size paper and display on your table. Or make a big overhead sign so people can see it from far away.

S7: Perfect Your Process

Session Length: 2 hours (variable)

Session Goals
- Create a Process Flow
- Create a Customer Experience
- Tweet About Your Product

Preparation
- Provide paper, pencils/pens, blunt scissors.

Options
- Invite a retail or food service expert.
- Additional Mentors OK in work segments.

7A. MAKE PROCESS SIGNS (40 mins)
- **Expert Presentation:** give tips on why signs are needed to direct customers.
- **Server to Lead:** Team Servers to lead creating Order, Pay and Pickup signs.

7B. DESIGN CUSTOMER PROCESS (40 mins)
- **Expert Presentation:** give tips & demo on how to create an efficient customer flow.
- **Server to Lead:** Team Servers to lead creating customer experience & flow.
- **Server to Present:** Servers to present and explain customer experience and flow.

---

7. Make Process Signs

Server: lead your team in creating process signs.

Your process signs should be displayed on your lemonade stand.

Order

Pay

Pickup

Perfect Your Process

Server: lead your team in creating a service process.

Main Sign?   Menu?   Ordering?   Extra Products?   Pay?   Pickup?

Draw sign locations to show where people will order, pay for and pickup products.

Name team members who will take orders, make the product, take the money and serve the product.

7C. TWEET ABOUT YOUR PRODUCT (40 mins)

- **Marketing Expert Presentation:** give tips & demo how to tweet about products.

- **Marketer to Lead:** Team Marketers to lead all in creating tweets.

- **Marketer to Present:** Marketers to present and explain.

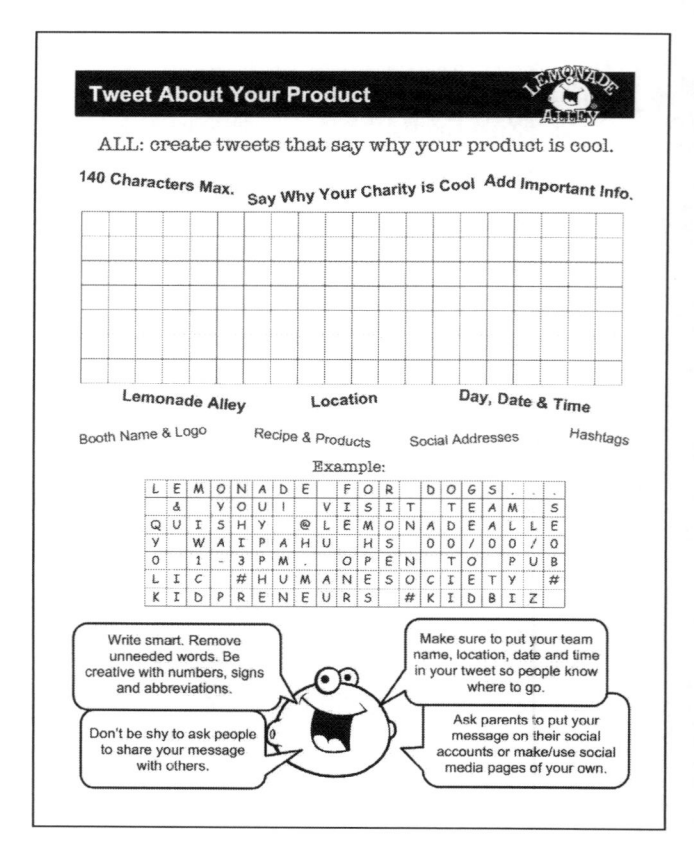

Tweet About Your Product

ALL: create tweets that say why your product is cool.

140 Characters Max.   Say Why Your Charity is Cool   Add Important Info.

Lemonade Alley — Location — Day, Date & Time
Booth Name & Logo — Recipe & Products — Social Addresses — Hashtags

Example:

L	E	M	O	N	A	D	E		F	O	R		D	O	G	S	.	.	.
	&		Y	O	U			V	I	S	I	T		T	E	A	M	S
Q	U	I	S	H	Y		@	L	E	M	O	N	A	D	E	A	L	L	E
Y		W	A	I	P	A	H	U		H	S		0	0	/	0	0	/	0
0		1	-	3	P	M	.		O	P	E	N		T	O		P	U	B
L	I	C		#	H	U	M	A	N	E	S	O	C	I	E	T	Y		#
K	I	D	P	R	E	N	E	U	R	S		#	K	I	D	B	I	Z	

- Write smart. Remove unneeded words. Be creative with numbers, signs and abbreviations.
- Make sure to put your team name, location, date and time in your tweet so people know where to go.
- Don't be shy to ask people to share your message with others.
- Ask parents to put your message on their social accounts or make/use social media pages of your own.

S8: Make Your Marketing

Session Length: 2 hours (variable)

Session Goals
- Create Posters & Flyers
- Make and Send an Invitation
- Tweet About Your Charity

Preparation
- Provide paper, pencils/pens, blunt scissors.

Options
- Invite a marketing expert.
- Additional Mentors OK in work segments.

8A. MAKE POSTERS (30 mins)
- **Expert Presentation:** give tips and demo how to create a great poster.
- **Provide Supplies:** provide paper and pens to teams.
- **Marketer to Lead:** Team Marketers to lead each team member making an advertising poster.

8B. MAKE FLYERS (30 mins)
- **Expert Presentation:** give tips and demo how to create a great flyer.
- **Provide Supplies:** provide paper and pens to teams.
- **Marketer to Lead:** Team Marketers to lead each team member making flyers.
- **Team Members to Present:** members to

8C. WRITE AN INVITATION (30 mins)

- **Marketing Expert Presentation:** give tips & demo how to make a great invite.

- **Marketer to Lead:** Team Marketers to lead all in creating letters.

- **Marketer to Present:** members to present and explain.

Create an Email or Letter Invitation

ALL: write an invitation to visit your team's stand:

List who should receive invitations:
Your Charity?   Parents?   Aunty/Uncle?   The Mayor?   Newscasters?

Make it easy and fun to read. And make sure to mention your charity.

Make sure to get your team name, location, date and time into your invitation so people know where to go!

8D. TWEET ABOUT YOUR PRODUCT (30 mins)

- **Marketing Expert Presentation:** give tips & demo how to tweet about charities.

- **Marketer to Lead:** Team Marketers to lead all in creating tweets.

- **Marketer to Present:** members to present and explain.

Tweet About Your Charity

ALL: create a tweet that highlights your charity.

140 Characters Max.   Say Why Your Charity is Cool   Add Important Info.

Lemonade Alley   Location   Day, Date & Time
Booth Name & Logo   Recipe & Products   Social Addresses   Hashtags

Example:

S	U	P	P	O	R	T		T	H	E		H	U	M	A	N	E		S
O	C	I	E	T	Y	.		V	I	S	I	T		T	E	A	M		S
Q	U	I	S	H	Y		@	L	E	M	O	N	A	D	E	A	L	L	E
Y		W	A	I	P	A	H	U		H	S		0	0	/	0	0	/	0
0		1	-	3	P	M	.		O	P	E	N		T	O		P	U	B
L	I	C		#	H	U	M	A	N	E	S	O	C	I	E	T	Y		#
K	I	D	P	R	E	N	E	U	R	S		#	K	I	D	B	I	Z	

Write smart. Remove unneeded words. Be creative with numbers, signs and abbreviations.

Make sure to put your team name, location, date and time in your tweet so people know where to go.

Don't be shy to ask people to share your message with others.

Ask parents to put your message on their social accounts or make/use social media pages of your own.

S9: Create a Sales Pitch

Session Length: 2 hours (variable)

Session Goals
- Create a 1-Minute Sales Pitch
- Create Media Interview Talk Points

Options
- Invite a drama or media expert.
- Additional Mentors OK in work segments.

9A. CREATE A SALES PITCH (60 mins)
- **Expert Presentation:** give tips and demo how to create a great sales pitch.
- **President to Lead:** Team Presidents to lead making a sales pitch.
- **Teams to Present:** have teams present their pitch to all.

9B. MAKE & PRACTICE TALK POINTS (60 mins)
- **Expert Presentation:** give tips and demo how to perform well in an interview including how to use the mic, what to say and how to behave.
- **Provide Supplies:** provide paper and pens to teams.
- **Marketer to Lead:** Team President to lead team in preparing talk points.
- **All Members Practice:** use mobile phones of

S10: Test, Tweak & Tweet

Session Length: 2 hours (variable)

Session Goals
- Check & Test All Items for Event
- Tweet About Upcoming Event

Options
- Invite charity representatives.

10A. CHECKLIST, TEST & TWEAK (90 mins)
- **President to Lead Checklist:** Team Presidents to lead checking off and perfecting all items needed for Lemonade Alley event.
- **Tweak All Items:** President, Treasurer, Maker, Marketer and Server should check all items.
- **Review Sales Pitch:** Teams to practice/perfect sales pitches.

10B. TWEET ABOUT YOUR EVENT (30 mins)
- **Marketer to Lead:** Team Marketers to lead all in creating tweets.

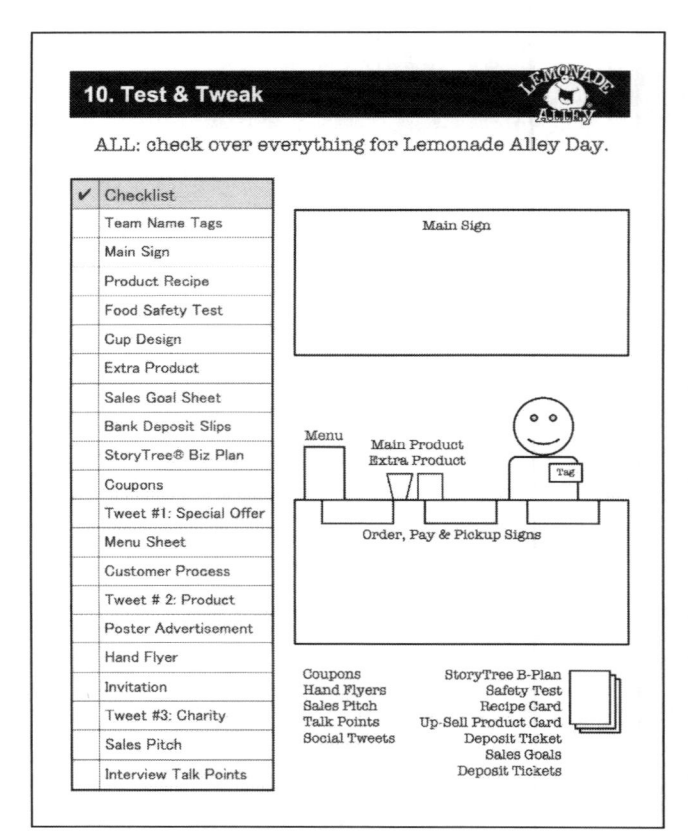

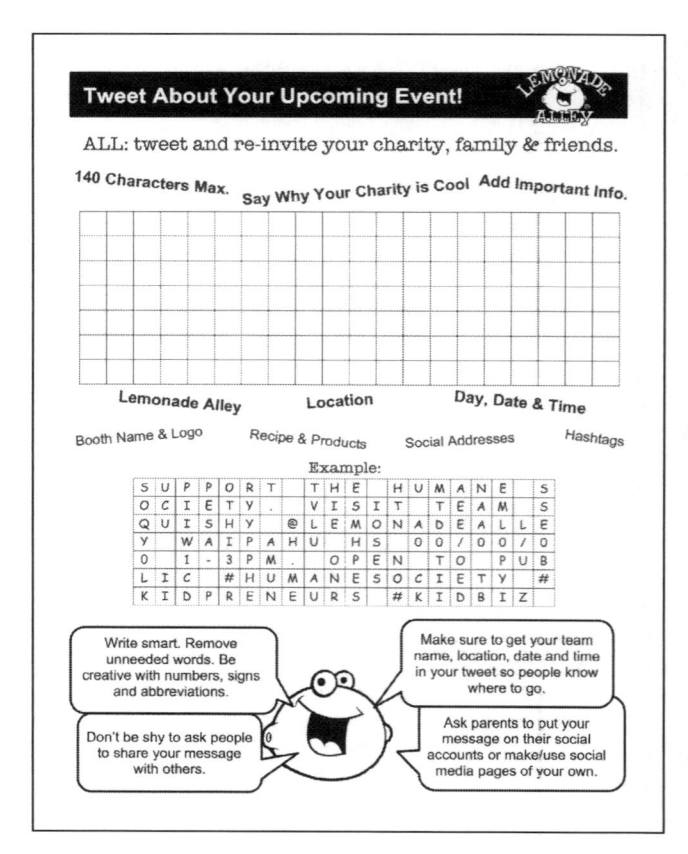

---

10. Test & Tweak

ALL: check over everything for Lemonade Alley Day.

✓	Checklist
	Team Name Tags
	Main Sign
	Product Recipe
	Food Safety Test
	Cup Design
	Extra Product
	Sales Goal Sheet
	Bank Deposit Slips
	StoryTree® Biz Plan
	Coupons
	Tweet #1: Special Offer
	Menu Sheet
	Customer Process
	Tweet # 2: Product
	Poster Advertisement
	Hand Flyer
	Invitation
	Tweet #3: Charity
	Sales Pitch
	Interview Talk Points

Tweet About Your Upcoming Event!

ALL: tweet and re-invite your charity, family & friends.

140 Characters Max. Say Why Your Charity is Cool Add Important Info.

Lemonade Alley — Location — Day, Date & Time
Booth Name & Logo — Recipe & Products — Social Addresses — Hashtags

Example:

S	U	P	P	O	R	T		T	H	E		H	U	M	A	N	E		S
O	C	I	E	T	Y	.		V	I	S	I	T		T	E	A	M		S
Q	U	I	S	H	Y		@	L	E	M	O	N	A	D	E	A	L	L	E
Y		W	A	I	P	A	H	U		H	S		0	0	/	0	0	/	0
0		1	-	3	P	M	.		O	P	E	N		T	O		P	U	B
L	I	C		#	H	U	M	A	N	E	S	O	C	I	E	T	Y		#
K	I	D	P	R	E	N	E	U	R	S		#	K	I	D	B	I	Z	

- Write smart. Remove unneeded words. Be creative with numbers, signs and abbreviations.
- Don't be shy to ask people to share your message with others.
- Make sure to get your team name, location, date and time in your tweet so people know where to go.
- Ask parents to put your message on their social accounts or make/use social media pages of your own.

S10

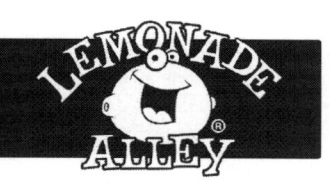

10C. EVENT DETAILS, Q & A (30 mins)

- **Explain Event Details:** Team Presidents to log details in Workbook details sheet.

- **Explain Prizes:** Prizes may be secured from local companies donating SWAG or other fun kid items. Grand prize of sending a winning team all expenses paid to a regional Lemonade Alley in Honolulu (based on Lemonade Tax collected at your local event).

- **Explain Judging:** you can choose how your local contest is judged. It can be by an expert panel, by audience favorite booth vote or any other means you like.

- **Take Questions:** answer all questions.

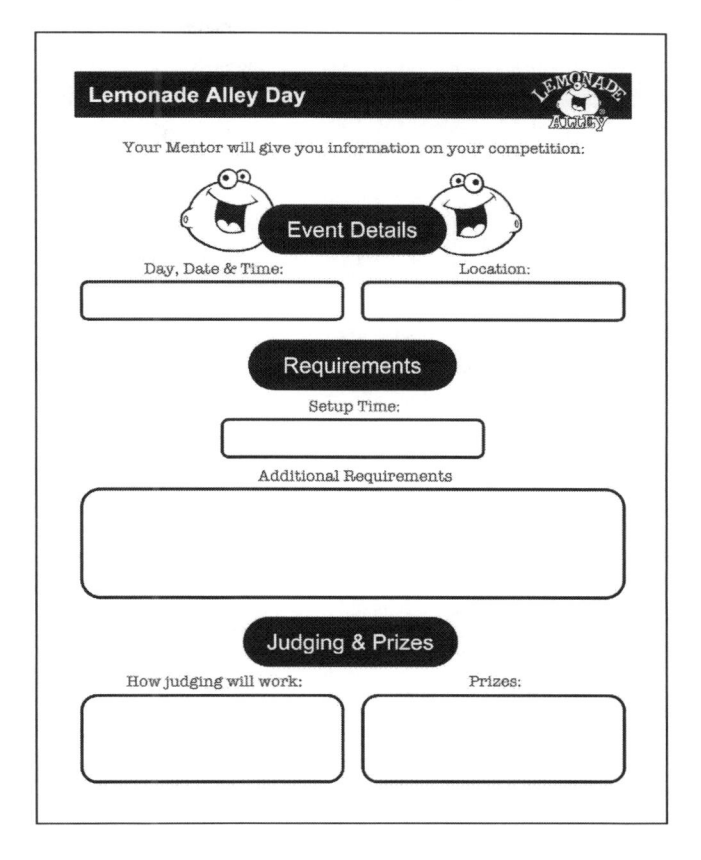

FORMS IN APPENDIX

- Note that clean forms are available at the end of the workbook.

Lemonade Alley Day

Your Mentor will give you information on your competition:

Event Details

Day, Date & Time:

Location:

Requirements

Setup Time:

Additional Requirements

Judging & Prizes

How judging will work:

Prizes:

Lemonade Alley Forms

Cut out the following forms for use on your lemonade stand:

Name Badges
Food Safety Certificate
Recipe Card
Up-Sell Product Card
Sales Performance
Bank Deposit Slips
StoryTree® Biz Plan
Sales Pitch Script
Interview Talk Points

Event Day Checklist

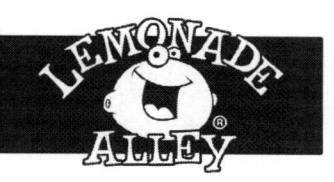

Use this Checklist to Run Your Event

Preparation Checklist

- [ ] **Scrip/Tickets:** exchange visitors' cash for tickets, typically 50 cents per ticket (scrip art at the end of this book).
- [ ] **Cash Box:** get a shoebox to keep cash, deposit tickets and forms. You might consider having a receipt book on hand for those wishing a receipt.
- [ ] **Voting Ticket:** provide some sort of best-of-show voting mechanism like a ticket per person to select a winning team.
- [ ] **Tables:** setup long cafeteria tables for teams to display signboards and serve lemonade. Allow 6' per team. Décor like yellow tablecloths helps the photo opp.
- [ ] **Lemonade:** provide dry mix or bottled lemonade for teams. You might get a sponsor to donate lemonade.
- [ ] **Garnishes:** provide small fruits, candies, umbrellas, etc. for teams to decorate product with. You can also allow teams to bring in food-safe garnish items.
- [ ] **Gloves & Plastic Knives:** provide sanitary and child-safe preparation items.
- [ ] **Tiny Cups:** provide the smallest cups possible (1-3 oz). Tasters are best as most visitors will want to support all teams and small reduces cost and waste.
- [ ] **Prizes:** try to get local companies to give small prizes and select winners for best healthy, local, fun, etc. awards. Gift cards, stickers and the like are fun and a motivating force for kids.

For Pictures & Ideas:
LemonadeAlley.com

Event Schedule

- [ ] **Hang Posters:** display team posters up to a week before your Lemonade Alley Day.
- [ ] **Team Setup:** have teams to setup 30-60 minutes before visitors are allowed to buy.
- [ ] **Open Sales:** allow visitors to purchase scrip and exchange for lemonade at team stands. Selling for 1-2 hours is enough to create a good selling experience.
- [ ] **Open Lemon Bank:** allow team Treasurers to use Deposit Tickets to add money and Best-of-Show voting tickets to their accounts. Keep track of money and voting by team.
- [ ] **End Sales & Collect Sales Sheets:** close sales and collect team sales sheets.
- [ ] **Tabulate & Cleanup:** start cleanup while sales and best-of-show voting are being calculated.
- [ ] **Award Prizes & Announce Results:** announce special prize winners, winning team and sales/donation results.

People Checklist

- [ ] **Scrip Seller:** someone to collect visitor cash and give scrip and best-of-show tickets.
- [ ] **Lemon Bank Teller:** someone to collect scrip deposits and receipts from teams and calculate distributions to charities.
- [ ] **Charity Rep.:** invite a representative to attend the event and accept donations.
- [ ] **Sponsor Rep.:** invite your school principal.
- [ ] **Press:** have charities or program sponsors invite TV/newspaper reporters and bloggers.

Tabulation Sheet

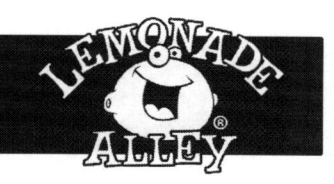

Enter Team Performance To Tabulate Results:

Team	Team Goal	Lemonade Sales	Extra Product	Tips & Donations	Team Total
1					
2					
3					
4					
5					
6					
7					
8					
9					
10					
11					
12					
13					
14					
15					
Page Totals					
Totals From Additional Pages					
Total Income	$	$	$	$	$

Profit to SHARE! (Calculate Charity Donation)	
Total Income	$
Percentage Donation to Charity	%
Total Donation (Total Income x % Donation)	$

Additional Tabulation Sheet

Enter Additional Teams:

Team	Team Goal	Lemonade Sales	Extra Product	Tips & Donations	Team Total
16					
17					
18					
19					
20					
21					
22					
23					
24					
25					
26					
27					
28					
29					
30					
31					
32					
33					
34					
35					
36					
37					
Page Totals	$	$	$	$	$

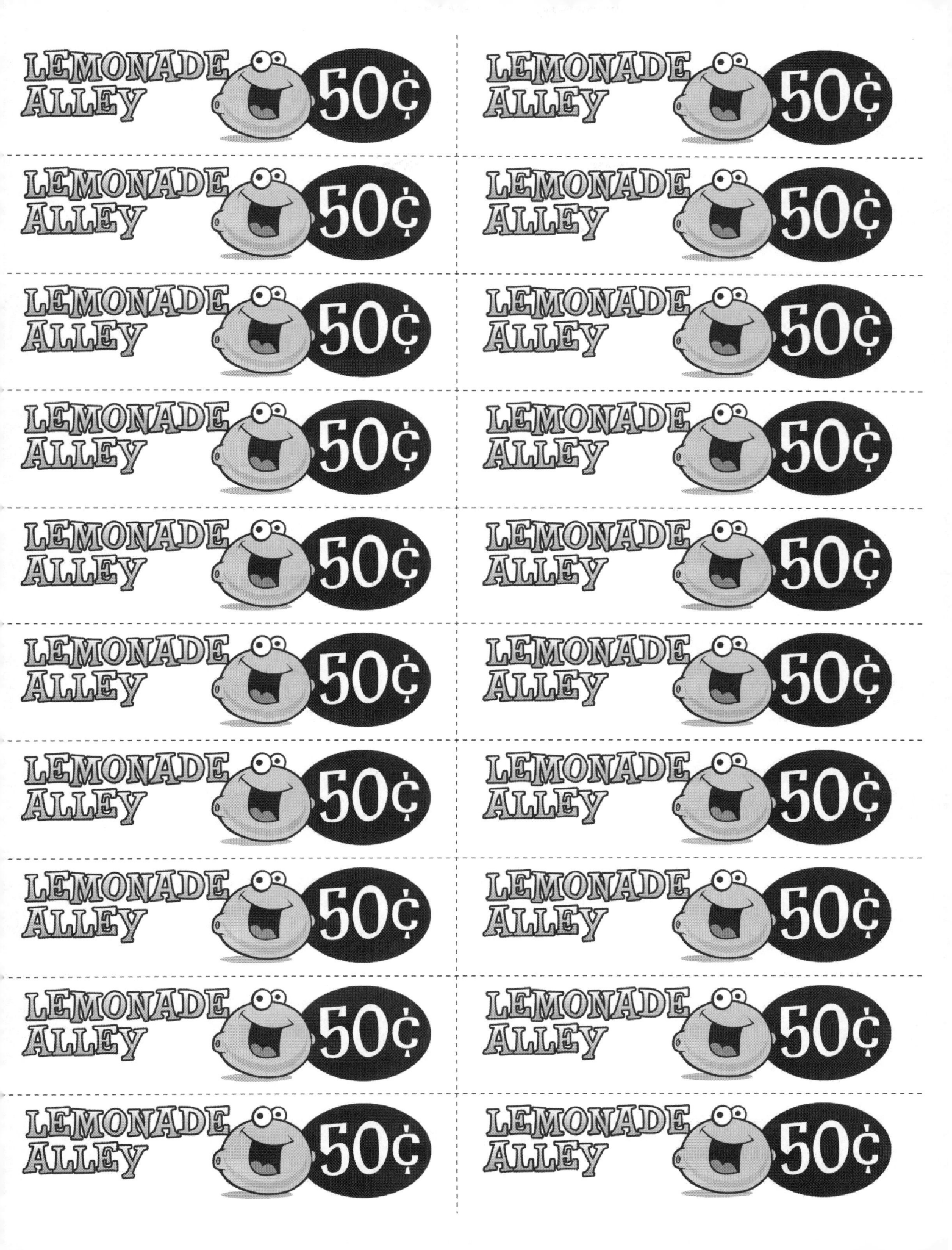

Made in the USA
Las Vegas, NV
04 June 2024